'I truly t[...]
I'd never make
it back.'

DANTE ALIGHIERI
Born 1265, Florence, Italy
Died 1321, Ravenna, Italy

Dante wrote the *Divina Commedia* between 1308 and 1321.
This selection of cantos is taken from *Inferno* translated by
Robin Kirkpatrick, Penguin Classics, 2006.

DANTE IN PENGUIN CLASSICS
Inferno
Purgatorio
Paradiso
The Divine Comedy
Vita Nuova

DANTE ALIGHIERI

Circles of Hell

Translated by
Robin Kirkpatrick

PENGUIN BOOKS

PENGUIN CLASSICS

Published by the Penguin Group
Penguin Books Ltd, 80 Strand, London WC2R ORL, England
Penguin Group (USA) Inc., 375 Hudson Street, New York, New York 10014, USA
Penguin Group (Canada), 90 Eglinton Avenue East, Suite 700, Toronto, Ontario,
Canada M4P 2Y3 (a division of Pearson Penguin Canada Inc.)
Penguin Ireland, 25 St Stephen's Green, Dublin 2, Ireland
(a division of Penguin Books Ltd)
Penguin Group (Australia), 707 Collins Street, Melbourne, Victoria 3008, Australia
(a division of Pearson Australia Group Pty Ltd)
Penguin Books India Pvt Ltd, 11 Community Centre, Panchsheel Park,
New Delhi – 110 017, India
Penguin Group (NZ), 67 Apollo Drive, Rosedale, Auckland 0632, New Zealand
(a division of Pearson New Zealand Ltd)
Penguin Books (South Africa) (Pty) Ltd, Block D, Rosebank Office Park,
181 Jan Smuts Avenue, Parktown North, Gauteng 2193, South Africa

Penguin Books Ltd, Registered Offices: 80 Strand, London WC2R ORL, England

www.penguin.com

This selection published in Penguin Classics 2015
002

Translation copyright © Robin Kirkpatrick, 2006

The moral right of the translator has been asserted

Set in 9/12.4 pt Baskerville 10 Pro
Typeset by Jouve (UK), Milton Keynes
Printed in Great Britain by Clays Ltd, St Ives plc

A CIP catalogue record for this book is available from the British Library

ISBN: 978-0-141-98022-5

www.greenpenguin.co.uk

Contents

Canto III

'Through me you go to the grief-wracked city.
Through me to everlasting pain you go.
Through me you go and pass among lost souls.
   Justice inspired my exalted Creator.
I am a creature of the Holiest Power,
of Wisdom in the Highest and of Primal Love.
   Nothing till I was made was made, only
eternal beings. And I endure eternally.
Surrender as you enter every hope you have.'
   These were the words that – written in dark tones –
I saw there, on the summit of a door.
I turned: 'Their meaning, sir, for me is hard.'
   And he in answering (as though he understood):
'You needs must here surrender all your doubts.
All taint of cowardice must here be dead.
   We now have come where, as I have said, you'll see
in suffering the souls of those who've lost
the good that intellect desires to win.'
   And then he placed his hand around my own,
he smiled, to give me some encouragement,
and set me on to enter secret things.
   Sighing, sobbing, moans and plaintive wailing
all echoed here through air where no star shone,
and I, as this began, began to weep.

Discordant tongues, harsh accents of horror,
tormented words, the twang of rage, strident
voices, the sound, as well, of smacking hands,

together these all stirred a storm that swirled
for ever in the darkened air where no time was,
as sand swept up in breathing spires of wind.

I turned, my head tight-bound in confusion,
to say to my master: 'What is it that I hear?
Who can these be, so overwhelmed by pain?'

'This baleful condition,' he said, 'is one
that grips those souls whose lives, contemptibly,
were void alike of honour and ill fame.

These all co-mingle with a noisome choir
of angels who – not rebels, yet not true
to God – existed for themselves alone.

To keep their beauty whole, the Heavens spurned them.
Nor would the depths of Hell receive them in,
lest truly wicked souls boast over them.'

And I: 'What can it be, so harsh, so heavy,
that draws such loud lamentings from these crowds?'
And he replied: 'My answer can be brief:

These have no hope that death will ever come.
And so degraded is the life they lead
all look with envy on all other fates.

The world allows no glory to their name.
Mercy and Justice alike despise them.
Let us not speak of them. Look, then pass on.'

I did look, intently. I saw a banner
running so rapidly, whirling forwards,
that nothing, it seemed, would ever grant a pause.

Drawn by that banner was so long a trail
of men and women I should not have thought
that death could ever have unmade so many.

A few I recognized. And then I saw –
and knew beyond all doubt – the shadow of the one
who made, from cowardice, the great denial.

So I, at that instant, was wholly sure
this congregation was that worthless mob
loathsome alike to God and their own enemies.

These wretched souls were never truly live.
They now went naked and were sharply spurred
by wasps and hornets, thriving all around.

The insects streaked the face of each with blood.
Mixing with tears, the lines ran down; and then
were garnered at their feet by filthy worms.

And when I'd got myself to look beyond,
others, I saw, were ranged along the bank
of some great stream. 'Allow me, sir,' I said,

'to know who these might be. What drives them on,
and makes them all (as far, in this weak light,
as I discern) so eager for the crossing?'

'That will, of course, be clear to you,' he said,
'when once our footsteps are set firm upon
the melancholic shores of Acheron.'

At this – ashamed, my eyes cast humbly down,
fearing my words had weighed on him too hard –
I held my tongue until we reached the stream.

Look now! Towards us in a boat there came
an old man, yelling, hair all white and aged,
'Degenerates! Your fate is sealed! Cry woe!

Don't hope you'll ever see the skies again!
I'm here to lead you to the farther shore,
into eternal shadow, heat and chill.

And you there! You! Yes, you, the living soul!
Get right away from this gang! These are dead.'
But then, on seeing that I did not move:

'You will arrive by other paths and ports.
You'll start your journey from a different beach.
A lighter hull must carry you across.'

'Charon,' my leader, 'don't torment yourself.
For this is willed where all is possible
that is willed there. And so demand no more.'

The fleecy wattles of the ferry man –
who plied across the liverish swamp, eyeballs
encircled by two wheels of flame – fell mute.

But not the other souls. Naked and drained,
their complexions changed. Their teeth began
(hearing his raw command) to gnash and grind.

They raged, blaspheming God and their own kin,
the human race, the place and time, the seed
from which they'd sprung, the day that they'd been born.

And then they came together all as one,
wailing aloud along the evil margin
that waits for all who have no fear of God.

Charon the demon, with his hot-coal eyes,
glared what he meant to do. He swept all in.
He struck at any dawdler with his oar.

In autumn, leaves are lifted, one by one,
away until the branch looks down and sees
its tatters all arrayed upon the ground.

In that same way did Adam's evil seed
hurtle, in sequence, from the river rim,
as birds that answer to their handler's call.

Then off they went, to cross the darkened flood.
And, long before they'd landed over there,
another flock assembled in their stead.

Attentively, my master said: 'All those,
dear son, who perish in the wrath of God,
meet on this shore, wherever they were born.

And they are eager to be shipped across.
Justice of God so spurs them all ahead
that fear in them becomes that sharp desire.

But no good soul will ever leave from here.
And so when Charon thus complains of you,
you may well grasp the sense that sounds within.'

His words now done, the desolate terrain
trembled with such great violence that the thought
soaks me once more in a terrified sweat.

The tear-drenched earth gave out a gust of wind,
erupting in a flash of bright vermilion,
that overwhelmed all conscious sentiment.

I fell like someone gripped by sudden sleep.

Canto V

THE LUSTFUL

And so from Circle One I now went down
deeper, to Circle Two, which bounds a lesser space
and therefore greater suffering. Its sting is misery.

Minos stands there – horribly there – and barking.
He, on the threshold, checks degrees of guilt,
then judges and dispatches with his twirling tail.

I mean that every ill-begotten creature,
when summoned here, confesses everything.
And he (his sense of sin is very fine)

perceives what place in Hell best suits each one,
and coils his tail around himself to tell
the numbered ring to which he'll send them down.

Before him, always, stands a crowd of souls.
By turns they go, each one, for sentencing.
Each pleads, attends – and then is tipped below.

'You there, arriving at this house of woe,'
so, when he saw me there, the judge spoke forth,
(to interrupt a while his formal role),

'watch as you enter – and in whom you trust.
Don't let yourself be fooled by this wide threshold.'
My leader's thrust: 'This yelling! Why persist?

Do not impede him on his destined way.
For this is willed where all is possible
that is willed there. And so demand no more.'

But now the tones of pain, continuing,

demand I hear them out. And now I've come
where grief and weeping pierce me at the heart.

And so I came where light is mute, a place
that moans as oceans do impelled by storms,
surging, embattled in conflicting squalls.

The swirling wind of Hell will never rest.
It drags these spirits onwards in its force.
It chafes them – rolling, clashing – grievously.

Then, once they reach the point from which they fell . . .
screams, keening cries, the agony of all,
and all blaspheming at the Holy Power.

Caught in this torment, as I understood,
were those who – here condemned for carnal sin –
made reason bow to their instinctual bent.

As starlings on the wing in winter chills
are borne along in wide and teeming flocks,
so on these breathing gusts the evil souls.

This way and that and up and down they're borne.
Here is no hope of any comfort ever,
neither of respite nor of lesser pain.

And now, as cranes go singing lamentations
and form themselves through air in long-drawn lines,
coming towards me, trailing all their sorrows,

I saw new shadows lifted by this force.
'Who are these people, sir?' I said. 'Tell me
why black air scourges them so viciously.'

'The first of those whose tale you wish to hear,'
he answered me without a moment's pause,
'governed as empress over diverse tongues.

She was so wracked by lust and luxury,

licentiousness was legal under laws she made –
to lift the blame that she herself incurred.

This is Semiramis. Of her one reads
that she, though heir to Ninus, was his bride.
Her lands were those where now the Sultan reigns.

The other, lovelorn, slew herself and broke
her vow of faith to Sichaeus's ashes.
And next, so lascivious, Cleopatra.

Helen. You see? Because of her, a wretched
waste of years went by. See! Great Achilles.
He fought with love until his final day.

Paris you see, and Tristan there.' And more
than a thousand shadows he numbered, naming
them all, whom Love had led to leave our life.

Hearing that man of learning herald thus
these chevaliers of old, and noble ladies,
pity oppressed me and I was all but lost.

'How willingly,' I turned towards the poet,
'I'd speak to those two there who go conjoined
and look to be so light upon the wind.'

And he to me: 'You'll see them clearer soon.
When they are closer, call to them. Invoke
the love that draws them on, and they will come.'

The wind had swept them nearer to us now.
I moved to them in words: 'Soul-wearied creatures!
Come, if none forbids, to us and, breathless, speak.'

As doves, when called by their desires, will come –
wings spreading high – to settle on their nest,
borne through the air by their own steady will,

so these two left the flock where Dido is.

They came, approaching through malignant air,
so strong for them had been my feeling cry.

'Our fellow being, gracious, kind and good!
You, on your journeying through this bruised air,
here visit two who tinged the world with blood.

Suppose the Sovereign of the Universe
were still our friend, we'd pray He grant you peace.
You pity so the ill perverting us.

Whatever you may please to hear or say,
we, as we hear, we, as we speak, assent,
so long – as now they do – these winds stay silent.

My native place is set along those shores
through which the river Po comes down, to be
at last at peace with all its tributaries.

Love, who so fast brings flame to generous hearts,
seized him with feeling for the lovely form,
now torn from me. The harm of how still rankles.

Love, who no loved one pardons love's requite,
seized me for him so strongly in delight
that, as you see, he does not leave me yet.

Love drew us onwards to consuming death.
Cain's ice awaits the one who quenched our lives.'
These words, borne on to us from them, were theirs.

And when I heard these spirits in distress,
I bowed my eyes and held them low, until,
at length, the poet said: 'What thoughts are these?'

I, answering in the end, began: 'Alas,
how many yearning thoughts, what great desire,
have led them through such sorrow to their fate?'

And turning to them now I came to say:

9

'Francesca, how your suffering saddens me!
Sheer pity brings me to the point of tears.

But tell me this: the how of it – and why –
that Love, in sweetness of such sighing hours,
permitted you to know these doubtful pangs.'

To me she said: 'There is no sorrow greater
than, in times of misery, to hold at heart
the memory of happiness. (Your teacher knows.)

And yet, if you so deeply yearn to trace
the root from which the love we share first sprang,
then I shall say – and speak as though in tears.

One day we read together, for pure joy
how Lancelot was taken in Love's palm.
We were alone. We knew no suspicion.

Time after time, the words we read would lift
our eyes and drain all colour from our faces.
A single point, however, vanquished us.

For when at last we read the longed-for smile
of Guinevere – at last her lover kissed –
he, who from me will never now depart,

touched his kiss, trembling to my open mouth.
This book was *Galehault* – pander-penned, the pimp!
That day we read no further down those lines.'

And all the while, as one of them spoke on,
the other wept, and I, in such great pity,
fainted away as though I were to die.

And now I fell as bodies fall, for dead.

Canto VI

THE GLUTTONOUS

As now I came once more to conscious mind –
closed in those feelings for the kindred souls
that had, in sudden sadness, overcome me –
    wherever I might turn I saw – wherever
I might move or send my gaze –
new forms of torment, new tormented souls.
    I am in Circle Three. And rain falls there,
endlessly, chill, accursed and heavy,
its rate and composition never new.
    Snow, massive hailstones, black, tainted water
pour down in sheets through tenebrae of air.
The earth absorbs it all and stinks, revoltingly.
    Cerberus, weird and monstrously cruel,
barks from his triple throats in cur-like yowls
over the heads of those who lie there, drowned.
    His eyes vermilion, beard a greasy black,
his belly broad, his fingers all sharp-nailed,
he mauls and skins, then hacks in four, these souls.
    From all of them, rain wrings a wet-dog howl.
They squirm, as flank screens flank. They twist, they turn,
and then – these vile profanities – they turn again.
    That reptile Cerberus now glimpsed us there.
He stretched his jaws; he showed us all his fangs.
And me? No member in my frame stayed still!
    My leader, bending with his palms wide-spanned,

11

scooped dirt in each, and then – his fists both full –
hurled these as sops down all three ravening throats.

A hungry mongrel – yapping, thrusting out,
intent on nothing but the meal to come –
is silent only when its teeth sink in.

In that same way, with three repulsive muzzles,
the demon Cerberus. His thunderous growlings
stunned these souls. They wished themselves stone deaf.

Over such shadows, flat in that hard rain,
we travelled onwards still. Our tread now fell
on voided nothings only seeming men.

Across the whole terrain these shades were spread,
except that one, at seeing us pass by,
sat, on the sudden, upright and then cried:

'You there! Drawn onwards through this stretch of Hell,
tell me you know me. Say so, if so you can.
You! Made as man before myself unmade.'

And I replied: 'The awful pain you feel
perhaps has cancelled you from memory.
Till now, it seems, I've never even seen you.

Then tell me who you are, and why you dwell
in such a place? And why a pain like this?
Others may well be worse, none so disgusting.'

And he: 'That burgh of yours – that sack of bile
that brims by now to overflow – I lived
as hers throughout my own fine-weather years.

You knew me, like your city friends, as Hoggo.
So here I am, condemned for gullet sins,
lying, you see, squashed flat by battering rain.

I'm not alone in misery of soul.

These all lie subject to the self-same pain.
Their guilt is mine.' He spoke no further word.

'Hoggo, your heavy labours,' I replied,
'weigh on me hard and prompt my heavy tears.
But tell me, if you can, where they'll all end,
   the citizens of that divided town?
Is there among them any honest man?
Why is that place assailed by so much strife?'

   His answer was: 'From each side, long harangues.
And then to blood. The Wildwood boys
will drive the others out. They'll do great harm.

   But then, within the span of three brief suns,
that side will fall and others rise and thrive,
spurred on by one who now just coasts between.

   For quite some time they'll hold their heads up high
and grind the others under heavy weights,
however much, for shame, these weep and writhe.

   Of this lot, two are honest yet not heard.
For pride and avarice and envy are
the three fierce sparks that set all hearts ablaze.'

   With this, his tear-drenched song now reached an end.
But I to him: 'I still want more instruction.
This gift I ask of you: please do say more.

   Tegghiaio, Farinata – men of rank –
Mosca, Arrigo, Rusticucci, too,
and others with their minds on noble deeds,

   tell me, so I may know them, where they are.
For I am gripped by great desire, to tell
if Heaven holds them sweet – or poisonous Hell.'

   And he: 'These dwell among the blackest souls,

loaded down deep by sins of differing types.
If you sink far enough, you'll see them all.

But when you walk once more where life is sweet,
bring me, I beg, to others in remembrance.
No more I'll say, nor answer any more.'

His forward gaze now twisted to a squint.
He stared at me a little, bent his head,
then fell face down and joined his fellow blind.

My leader now addressed me: 'He'll not stir
until the trumpets of the angels sound,
at which his enemy, True Power, will come.

Then each will see once more his own sad tomb,
and each, once more, assume its flesh and figure,
each hear the rumbling thunder roll for ever.'

So on we fared across that filthy blend
of rain and shadow spirit, slow in step,
touching a little on the life to come.

Concerning which, 'These torments, sir,' I said,
'when judgement has been finally proclaimed –
will these increase or simmer just the same?'

'Return,' he said, 'to your first principles:
when anything (these state) becomes more perfect,
then all the more it feels both good and pain.

Albeit these accursed men will not
achieve perfection full and true, they still,
beyond that Day, will come to sharper life.'

So, circling on the curve around that path,
we talked of more than I shall here relate,
but reached the brow, from which the route descends,
    and found there Plutus, the tremendous foe.

Canto VIII

THE WRATHFUL AND THE
MELANCHOLIC

And so I say (continuing) that, long before
we reached the bottom of that lofty tower,
our eyes had travelled upwards to its summit,

   drawn by a pair of tiny flames, set there –
as now we saw – to signal to a third,
so far away the eye could hardly grasp it.

   I turned towards the ocean of all wisdom:
'What do they mean?' I said to him. 'What answer
follows from the farther fire? Who makes these signs?'

   And he: 'Across these waves of foaming mire,
you may already glimpse what they've been waiting for,
unless it still goes hidden by these marshy fumes.'

   No bow string ever shot through air an arrow
rapider than now, at speed, I saw come on
towards us there, a mean little vessel,

   within it – as pilot plying these waters –
a single galley man who strained the oar,
squealing: 'You fiend! You've got it coming now!'

   'Phlegyas, Phlegyas!' my master said.
'Your screams and shouts have, this time, little point.
We're yours – but only while we cross this marsh.'

   Like someone hearing that a massive hoax
has just, to his disgruntlement, been pulled on him,
so Phlegyas now stood, in pent-up rage.

My lord stepped down, and, entering the boat,
he made me, in my turn, embark behind.
The hull seemed laden only when I did.

At once – my leader boarded, me as well –
the ancient prow put out. It sawed the waves
more deeply than it would with other crews.

So, rushing forwards on that lifeless slick,
there jerked up, fronting me, one brimming slime
who spoke: 'So who – you come too soon! – are you?'

And my riposte: 'I come, perhaps; I'll not remain.
But who might you be, brutishly befouled?'
His answer was: 'Just look at me. I'm one

who weeps.' And I to him: 'Weep on. In grief,
may you remain, you spirit of damnation!
I know who *you* are, filth as you may be.'

And then he stretched both hands towards our gunwales.
My teacher, though – alert – soon drove him back,
saying: 'Get down! Be off with all that dog pack!'

And then he ringed both arms around my neck.
He kissed my face, then said: 'You wrathful soul!
Blessed the one that held you in her womb.

That man, alive, flaunted his arrogance,
and nothing good adorns his memory.
So here his shadow is possessed with rage.

How many, in the world above, pose there
as kings but here will lie like pigs in muck,
leaving behind them horrible dispraise.'

'Sir,' I replied, 'this I should really like:
before we make our way beyond this lake,
to see him dabbled in the minestrone.'

He gave me my answer: 'Before that shore
has come to view, you'll surely have your fill.
And rightly you rejoice in this desire.'

Then, moments on, I saw that sinner ripped
to vicious tatters by that mud-caked lot.
I praise God still, and still give thanks for that.

'Get him,' they howled. 'Let's get him – Silver Phil!'
That crazy Florentine! He bucked, he baulked.
Turning, the Guelf turned teeth upon himself.

We left him there. Of him, my story tells no more.
And yet my ears were pierced with cries of pain.
At which, I barred my eyes intently forwards.

'Dear son,' my teacher in his goodness said,
'we now approach the city known as Dis,
its teeming crowds and weighty citizens.'

'Already, sir,' I said, 'I clearly can
make out the minarets beyond this moat,
as bright and red, it seems, as if they sprang

from fire.' 'Eternal fire,' he answered me,
'burning within, projects, as you can see,
these glowing profiles from the depths of Hell.'

We now arrived within the deep-dug ditch –
the channel round that place disconsolate,
whose walls, it seemed to me, were formed of iron.

Not without, first, encircling it about,
we came to where the ferry man broke forth:
'Out you all get!' he yelled. 'The entry's here.'

I saw there, on that threshold – framed – more than
a thousand who had rained from Heaven. Spitting
in wrath. 'Who's that,' they hissed, 'who, yet undead,

17

travels the kingdom of the truly dead?'
He gave a sign, my teacher in all wisdom,
saying he sought some secret word with them.

At which they somewhat hid their fierce disdain.
'You come, but on your own!' they said. 'Let him,
so brazen entering our realm, walk by.

He may retrace his foolish path alone –
or try it, if he can – while you'll stay here.
You've been his escort through this dark terrain.'

Reader, imagine! I grew faint at heart,
to hear these cursed phrases ringing out.
I truly thought I'd never make it back.

'My guide, my dearest master. Seven times –
or more by now – you've brought me safely through.
You've drawn me from the face of towering doom.

Do not, I beg you, leave me here undone.
If we are now denied a clear way on,
then let us quickly trace our footsteps back.'

My lord had led me onwards to that place –
and now he said: 'Do not be terrified.
No one can take from us our right to pass.

Wait here a while. Refresh your weary soul.
Take strength. Be comforted. Feed on good hope.
I'll not desert you in this nether world.'

So off he went. He there abandoned me,
my sweetest father. Plunged in 'perhapses',
I so remained, brain arguing 'yes' and 'no'.

What he then said to them I could not tell.
Yet hardly had he taken up his stand
when all ran, jostling, to return inside.

They barred the door, these enemies of ours,
to meet his thrust. My lord remained shut out.
With heavy tread, he now came back to me.

Eyes bent upon the ground, his forehead shaved
of all brave confidence, sighing, he said:
'Who dares deny me entrance to this house of grief?'

To me he said: 'You see. I'm angry now.
Don't be dismayed. They'll fuss around in there.
They'll seek to keep us out. But I'll win through.

This insolence of theirs is nothing new.
At some less secret gate they tried it once.
But that still stands without its lock, ajar.

You've seen the door, dead words scribed on its beam.
And now already there descends the slope –
passing these circles, and without a guide –

someone through whom the city will lie open.'

Canto XIII

THE VIOLENT AGAINST SELF

No, Nessus had not reached the other side
when we began to travel through a wood
that bore no sign of any path ahead.

No fresh green leaves but dismal in colour,
no boughs clean arc-ed but knotty and entwined,
no apples were there but thorns, poison-pricked.

No scrubby wilderness so bitter and dense
from Cécina as far as Corneto
offers a den to beasts that hate ploughed farmlands.

Their nest is there, those disgusting Harpies
who drove the Trojans from the Strophades,
with grim announcements of great harm to come.

Wings widespreading, human from neck to brow,
talons for feet, plumage around their paunches,
they sing from these uncanny trees their songs of woe.

Constant in kindness, my teacher now said:
'Before you venture further in, please know
that you now stand in Sub-ring Number Two,

and shall until you reach the Appalling Sands.
So look around. Take care. What you'll see here
would drain belief from any word I uttered.'

A wailing I heard, dragged out from every part,
and saw there no one who might make these sounds,
so that I stopped, bewildered, in my tracks.

Truly I think he truly thought that, truly,

I might just have believed these voices rose
from persons hidden from us in the thorn maze.

Therefore: 'If you,' my teacher said, 'will wrench
away some sprig from any tree you choose,
that will lop short your feeling in such doubt.'

And so I reached my hand a little forwards.
I plucked a shoot (no more) from one great hawthorn.
At which its trunk screamed out: 'Why splinter me?'

Now darkened by a flow of blood, the tree
spoke out a second time: 'Why gash me so?
Is there no living pity in your heart?

Once we were men. We've now become dry sticks.
Your hand might well have proved more merciful
if we had been the hissing souls of snakes.'

Compare: a green brand, kindled at one end –
the other oozing sap – whistles and spits
as air finds vent, then rushes out as wind.

So now there ran, out of this fractured spigot,
both words and blood. At which I let the tip
drop down and stood like someone terror-struck.

'You injured soul!' my teacher (sane as ever)
now replied. 'If he had only earlier
believed what my own writings could have shown,

he'd not have stretched his hand so far towards you.
This, though, is all beyond belief. So I was forced
to urge a deed that presses on my own mind still.

But tell him now who once you were. He may,
in turn, as remedy, refresh your fame,
returning to the world above by leave.'

The trunk: 'Your words, sir, prove so sweet a bait,

I cannot here keep silence. Don't be irked
if I a while should settle on that lure and talk.

    I am the one who held in hand both keys
to Federigo's heart. I turned them there,
locking so smoothly and unlocking it

    that all men, almost, I stole from his secrets.
Faith I kept, so true in that proud office
I wasted sleep and lost my steady pulse.

    That harlot Scandal, then (her raddled eyes
she never drags from where the emperor dwells,
the vice of court life, mortal blight of all)

    enflamèd the minds of everyone against me.
And they in flames enflamed the great Augustus.
So, happy honours turned to hapless grief.

    My mind – itself disdainful in its tastes –
believing it could flee disdain by dying,
made me unjust against myself so just.

    By all these weird, new-wooded roots, I swear
on oath before you: I did not break faith,
nor failed a lord so worthy of regard.

    Will you – should either head back to the world –
bring comfort to my memory, which lies
still lashed beneath the stroke of envious eyes?'

    Pausing a while, he said (my chosen poet),
'He's silent now, so waste no opportunity.
If there is more you wish to know, then say.'

    'You,' I replied, 'must speak once more and ask
what you believe will leave me satisfied.
I could not do it. Pity wrings my core.'

    And so he did once more begin: 'Suppose

that freely, from a generous heart, someone
should do, imprisoned ghost, what your prayers seek,

    tell us, if you should care to, this: how souls
are bound in these hard knots. And, if you can:
will anyone be ever loosed from limbs like these?'

    At that (exhaling heavily) the trunk
converted wind to word and formed this speech:
'The answer you require is quick to give:

    When any soul abandons savagely
its body, rending self by self away,
Minos consigns it to the seventh gulf.

    Falling, it finds this copse. Yet no one place
is chosen as its plot. Where fortune slings it,
there (as spelt grains might) it germinates.

    A sapling sprouts, grows ligneous, and then
the Harpies, grazing on its foliage,
fashion sharp pain and windows for that pain.

    We (as shall all), come Judgement Day, shall seek
our cast-off spoil, yet not put on this vestment.
Keeping what we tore off would not be fair.

    Our bodies we shall drag back here; and all
around this melancholy grove they'll swing,
each on the thorn of shades that wrought them harm.'

    Attention trained entirely on that stock
(thinking, in truth, it might as yet say more),
we now were shocked by a sudden uproar,

    as if (to make comparison) you'd heard some hog
and all the boar hunt baying round its stand –
a sound composed of beasts and thrashing twigs.

    And look there, on the left-hand side, there came,

at speed, two fleeing, naked, scratched to bits,
who broke down every hurdle in that scrub.

One was ahead: 'Quick, quick! Come, death! Come now!'
The other (seeming, to himself, too slow)
was yelling: 'Lano! Oh, your nimble heels
    weren't half so sharp at the Toppo rumble!'
And then (it may be his breath was failing),
he sank to form a clump beside a shrub.

Behind these two, the wood was teeming, full
of black bitches, ravenous and rapid,
as greyhounds are when slipping from their leads.

These set their teeth on that sad, hunkered form.
They tore him all to pieces, chunk by chunk.
And then they carried off those suffering limbs.

My guide then took me gently by the hand,
and led me to the bush, which wept (in vain)
through all of its blood-stained lacerations,

    saying: 'O Jacopo da Santo Andrea!
What use was it to take me as your shield?
Am I to blame for your wild, wicked ways?'

My teacher came and stood above that bush.
'So who were you,' he said, 'who, pierced to bits,
breathes painful utterance in jets of blood?'

'You souls,' he said, 'you come – but just in time –
to see the massacre, in all its shame,
that rends away from me my fresh green fronds.

Place all these leaves beneath this grieving stump.
I too was from that city, once, which chose
Saint John as patron over Mars – its first –
    whose arts, since spurned, have always brought us harm.

And were there not, beneath the Arno bridge,
some traces visible of what he was,
    those citizens who built it all anew
on ashes that Attila left behind
would then have laboured with no end in view.
    Myself, I made a gallows of my house.'

Canto XVII

'Behold! The beast who soars with needle tail
through mountains, shattering shields and city walls!
Behold! The beast that stinks out all the world!'
    To me, my lord spoke thus, then beckoned up
the monster to approach the jutting prow
that marked the end of all our marble paths.
    It came, that filthy image of deceit.
Its head and trunk it grounded on the shore.
It did not draw its tailpiece to the bank.
    The face was that of any honest man,
the outer skin all generosity.
Its timber, though, was serpent through and through:
    two clawing grabs, and hairy to the armpits,
its back and breast and ribcage all tattooed
with knot designs and spinning little whorls.
    No Turk or Tartar has woven finer drapes,
more many-coloured in their pile or tuft.
Nor did Arachne thread such tapestries.
    Compare: on foreshores, sometimes, dinghies stand
in water partly, partly on the shingle –
as likewise, in the land of drunken Germans,
    beavers will do, advancing their attack.
So did this beast – the worst that there can be –
there on the rocky rim that locks the sand.
    Out into emptiness it swung its tail,

and twisted upwards its venomous fork.
The tip was armed like any scorpion's.

My leader said: 'We need to bend our path
a little further down, towards that vile
monstrosity that's lolling underneath.'

So down we went, towards the right-hand pap.
Ten paces, and we'd reached the very edge,
stepping well clear of flames and burning shoals.

And then, on getting to that spot, I saw,
a little further on along the sandbar,
a group just sitting near the gaping waste.

And here my teacher said: 'To carry back
experience of the ring that we're now in,
go over there and look at their behaviour.

But do not stay to talk at any length.
Till you return, I'll parley with this thing,
for him to grant us use of his great thews.'

So once again, along the outward brow
of Circle Seven I progressed alone
to where there sat these souls in misery.

The pain they felt erupted from their eyes.
All up and down and round about, their hands
sought remedies for burning air and ground.

Dogs in the heat of summer do the same,
stung by the bluebottle, gadfly and flea,
swatting at swarms with paw pads or with snout.

On some of these – these faces under showers
of grievous, never-ceasing rain – I set my eyes.
I recognized no single one, but noticed
round the neck of each a cash bag hung

(each with its own insignia and blaze),
on which their staring eyes appeared to graze.

So I, too, gazing, passed among them all,
and saw, imprinted on a yellow purse,
a blue device, in face and pose a lion.

Then, as my view went trundling further on,
I saw another, with a blood-red field –
the goose it bore was whiter, far, than butter.

And then I heard (from one whose neat, white sack
was marked in azure with a pregnant sow):
'What are you after in this awful hole?

Do go away! Yet you – as Vitaliano is –
are still alive. Then understand me, please:
he'll sit on my left flank, my one-time neighbour.

I'm Paduan, among these Florentines,
and often they all thunder in my ears:
"Oh, let him come," they'll scream, "that sovereign knight,

who'll bring the bag that bears three rampant goats."'
At which, in throes, he wrenched his mouth awry
and curled his tongue, like any ox, to lick his nose.

And I, who feared that, if I lingered long,
I'd irritate the one who'd said 'Be brief',
now turned my back upon these worn-out souls.

My leader, I discovered there, had jumped
already on that fearsome creature's rump.
'Come on,' he urged, 'be stalwart and courageous.

From now on we'll descend by stairs like these.
Mount at the front so I can come between,
to see the tail won't bring you any harm.'

Like someone shivering as the grip of 'flu

spreads over him, pale to the fingernails,
who trembles merely at the sight of shade . . .

    well, that was me, as these words carried over.
The threat of shame, however, when one's lord
is near, emboldens one to serve him well.

    I settled down between those gruesome shoulders.
I wished to say (my voice, though, would not come):
'Yes. Please! Be sure you hold me very firm.'

    He, who in many an earlier 'perhaps'
had aided me, as soon as I got on,
flinging his arms around me, hugged me tight,

    and said: 'Go on, then, Geryon. Cast out!
Wheel wide about to make a smooth descent.
Think of the strange new burden on your back.'

    Slowly astern, astern, as ferries leave
the quay where they had docked, so he moved out.
Then, only when he felt himself ride free,

    he turned the tail where breast had been before,
and – stretching long, as eels might do – set sail,
paddling the air towards him with his paws.

    No greater fear (so, truly, I believe)
was felt as Phaeton let the reins go loose,
and scorched the sky as still it is today,

    nor yet by ill-starred Icarus – his loins
unfeathering as the wax grew warm – to whom
his father screamed aloud: 'You're going wrong!'

    And then with fear I saw, on every side,
that I was now in air, and every sight
extinguished, save my view of that great beast.

    So swimming slowly, it goes on its way.

It wheels. It descends. This I don't notice –
except an upward breeze now fans my face.

By then I heard, beneath us to the right,
the roar of some appalling cataract.
And so I leant my head out, looking down.

More timorous of falling still, I saw
that there were fires down there and heard shrill screams.
Trembling, I huddled back and locked my thighs.

And then I saw, as I had not before,
the going-down – the spirals of great harm –
on every side now coming ever nearer.

A falcon, having long been on the wing,
and seeing neither lure nor bird to prey on,
compels the falconer to sigh: 'You're coming in,'

then sinks down wearily to where it left so fast.
A hundred turns – and then, far from its lord,
it lands, disdainful, spiteful in its scorn.

So, too, did Geryon, to place us on the floor,
the very foot of that sheer, towering cliff.
And then, unburdened of our persons now,

vanished at speed like barbed bolt from a bow.

Canto XIX

You! Magic Simon, and your sorry school!
Things that are God's own – things that, truly, are
the brides of goodness – lusting cruelly
    after gold and silver, you turn them all to whores.
The trumpet now (and rightly!) sounds for you.
There you all are, well set in Pocket Three.

    Onwards towards this yawning tomb, mounting
the ridge, by now we'd reached its summit –
the point that plumbs the middle of the ditch.

    O wisdom in the height, how great the art
that you display in Heaven, on earth and even
in that evil world! How justly you deal power!

    I saw how all the livid rock was drilled
with holes – along its flanks, across its floor –
all circular, and all of equal measure.

    To me they seemed, in radius, no more nor less
than fonts that, in my own beloved Saint John's,
allow the priest at baptisms a place to stand.

    (Not long ago, I shattered one of those.
Someone was drowning there. I got them out.
This, sealed and sworn, is nothing but the truth.)

    Out of the mouth of every single hole
there floated up a pair of sinner feet,
legs to the ham on show, the rest concealed.

    The soles of all these feet were set alight,

and each pair wriggled at the joint so hard
they'd easily have ripped a rope or lanyard.

As flames go flickering round some greasy thing
and hover just above its outer rind,
so these flames also, toe tip to heel end.

'Who, sir,' I said, 'is that one there? That one
who jerks in pain greater than his *confrères*,
sucked at by flames far more fiercely vermilion.'

'I'll lift you down,' he answered me, 'if you
insist. We'll take that bank the easier.
He'll talk to you himself about his twists.'

'Whatever pleases you,' I said, 'to me is good.
Lord, you remain: I'll not depart – you know –
from what you will. You read my silent thoughts.'

So on we went to the fourth embankment.
We turned around, descended on our left,
arriving at that pitted, straitened floor.

My teacher, kindly, did not set me down –
nor loose me from his hip hold – till we had reached
that fissure where (all tears) shanks shuddered.

'Whatever you might be there, upside down,
staked, you unhappy spirit, like a pole,
if you,' I said, 'are able, then speak out.'

So there I stood like any friar who shrives
the hired assassin – head down in the earth –
who calls him back to put off stifling death.

And he yelled out: 'Is that you standing there?
Are you there, on your feet still, Boniface?
The writings lied to me by quite some years.

Are you so sick of owning things already?

Till now, you've hardly been afraid to cheat
our lovely woman, tearing her to shreds.'

　　Well, I just stood there (you will know just how)
simply not getting what I'd heard come out,
feeling a fool, uncertain what to say.

　　Then Virgil entered: 'Say this – and make speed:
"No, that's not me. I am not who you think."'
And so I answered as he'd said I should.

　　At which – all feet – the spirit thrashed about,
then, sighing loudly in a tearful voice:
'So what is it you want of me?' he said.

　　'If you're so keen to know who I might be,
and ran all down that slope to find me out,
you'd better know I wore the papal cope.

　　A true Orsini, son of Ursa Bear,
I showed such greed in favouring her brats
that – up there well in pocket – I'm in pocket here.

　　Below me, in great stacks beneath my head,
packed tight in every cranny of the rock,
are all my antecedents in the Simon line.

　　Down there I'll sink, in that same way, when he
arrives whom I supposed that you might be,
and uttered, therefore, my abrupt inquiry.

　　But I already – feet up on the grill, tossed
upside down – have passed more time
than Boniface will, stuck here with red hot toes.

　　For after him from westwards there'll appear
that lawless shepherd, uglier in deed,
who then, for both of us, will form a lid.

　　He shall be known as a "Jason-Once-Again".

We read in Maccabees: "Priest Bribes a King."
This other will score well with one French prince.'

    I may have been plain mad. I do not know.
But now, in measured verse, I sang these words:
'Tell me, I pray: what riches did Our Lord

    demand, as first instalment, from Saint Peter
before He placed the keys in his command?
He asked (be sure) no more than: "Come behind me."

    Nor did Saint Peter, or the rest of them,
receive from Matthias a gold or silver piece,
allotting him the place that Judas lost.

    So you stay put. You merit punishment.
But keep your eye on that ill-gotten coin
that made you bold with Charles the Angevin.

    And, were I not forbidden, as I am,
by reverence for those keys, supreme and holy,
that you hung on to in the happy life,

    I now would bring still weightier words to bear.
You and your greed bring misery to the world,
trampling the good and raising up the wicked.

    Saint John took heed of shepherds such as you.
He saw revealed that She-above-the-Waves,
whoring it up with Rulers of the earth,

    she who in truth was born with seven heads
and fed herself, in truth, from ten pure horns,
as long as she in virtue pleased her man.

    Silver and gold you have made your god. And what's
the odds – you and some idol-worshipper?
He prays to one, you to a gilded hundred.

    What harm you mothered, Emperor Constantine!

Not your conversion but the dowry he –
that first rich Papa – thus obtained from you!'
    And all the time I chanted out these notes,
he, in his wrath or bitten by remorse,
flapped, with great force, the flat of both his feet.
    My leader, I believe, was very pleased.
In listening to these sounding words of truth,
he stood there satisfied, his lips compressed.
    So, too, he took me up in his embrace.
Then, bodily, he clasped me to his breast
and climbed again the path where he'd come down.
    Nor did he tire of holding me so tight.
He bore me to the summit of that arch
spanning the banks of Pockets Four and Five.
    And there he gently put his burden down,
gently on rocks so craggy and so steep
they might have seemed to goats too hard to cross.
    From there, another valley was disclosed.

Canto XXIV

In that still baby-boyish time of year,
when sunlight chills its curls beneath Aquarius,
when nights grow shorter equalling the day,

   and hoar frost writes fair copies on the ground
to mimic in design its snowy sister
(its pen, though, not chill-tempered to endure),

   the peasant in this season, when supplies
run short, rolls from his bed, looks out and sees
the fields are glistening white, so slaps his thigh,

   goes in, then grumbles up and down, as though
(poor sod) he couldn't find a thing to do,
till, out once more, he fills his wicker trug,

   with hope, at least. No time at all! The features
of the world transform. He grabs his goad.
Outdoors, he prods his lambs to open pasture.

   In some such way, I too was first dismayed
to see distress so written on my leader's brow.
But he, as quickly, plastered up the hurt.

   And so, arriving at the ruined bridge,
my leader turned that sour-sweet look on me
that first he'd shown me at the mountain foot.

   He spread his arms, then, having in his thought
surveyed the landslip, and (a man of sense)
assessed it well, he took me in his grip.

   Then, always with adjustments in his moves

(so that, it seemed, he foresaw everything),
in hauling me towards the pinnacle

  of one moraine, he'd see a spur beyond
and say: 'Next, take your hold on that niche there.
But test it first to see how well it bears.'

  This was no route for someone warmly dressed.
Even for us – he, weightless, shoving me –
we hardly could progress from ledge to ledge.

  Had not the gradient been less severe
than that which faced it on the other side,
I'd have been beat. I cannot speak for him.

  But Rottenpockets slopes towards the flap
that opens on the lowest sump of all,
and so, in contour, every ditch is shaped

  with one rim proud, the other dipping down.
So, in the end, we came upon the point
where one last building block had sheared away.

  My lungs by now had so been milked of breath
that, come so far, I couldn't make it further.
I flopped, in fact, when we arrived, just there.

  'Now you must needs,' my teacher said, 'shake off
your wonted indolence. No fame is won
beneath the quilt or sunk in feather cushions.

  Whoever, fameless, wastes his life away,
leaves of himself no greater mark on earth
than smoke in air or froth upon the wave.

  So upwards! On! And vanquish laboured breath!
In any battle mind power will prevail,
unless the weight of body loads it down.

  There's yet a longer ladder you must scale.

You can't just turn and leave all these behind.
You understand? Well, make my words avail.'

So up I got, pretending to more puff
than, really, I could feel I'd got within.
'Let's go,' I answered, 'I'm all strength and dash.'

Upwards we made our way, along the cliff –
poor, narrow-going where the rocks jut out,
far steeper than the slope had been before.

Talking (to seem less feeble) on I went,
when, issuing from the ditch beyond, there came
a voice – though one unfit for human words.

I made no sense of it. But now I neared
the arch that forms a span across that pocket.
The speaker seemed much moved by raging ire.

Downwards I bent. But in such dark as that,
no eye alive could penetrate the depths.
But, 'Sir,' I said, 'make for the other edge,

and let us then descend the pocket wall.
From here I hear but do not understand.
So, too, I see, yet focus not at all.'

'I offer you,' he said to me, 'no answer
save "just do it". Noble demands, by right,
deserve the consequence of silent deeds.'

So where the bridgehead meets Embankment Eight
we then went down, pursuing our descent,
so all that pocket was displayed to me.

And there I came to see a dreadful brood
of writhing reptiles of such diverse kinds
the memory drains the very blood from me.

Let Libya boast – for all her sand – no more!

Engender as she may chelydri, pharae,
chenchres and amphisbaenae, jaculi,
   never – and, yes, add Ethiopia, too,
with all, beyond the Red Sea, dry and waste –
has she displayed so many vicious pests.
   And through all this abundance, bitter and grim,
in panic naked humans ran – no holes
to hide in here or heliotropic charms.
   Behind their backs, the sinners' hands were bound
by snakes. These sent both tail and neck between
the buttocks, then formed the ends in knots up front.
   And near our point, at one of them (just look!)
a serpent headlong hurled itself and pierced
exactly at the knit of spine and nape.
   Then, faster than you scribble 'i' or 'o',
that shape caught fire, flash-flared and then (needs must)
descended in cascading showers of ash.
   There, lying in destruction on the ground,
the dead dust gathered of its own accord,
becoming instantly the self it was.
   Compare: the phoenix (as the sages say)
will come to its five-hundredth year, then die,
but then, on its own pyre, be born anew.
   Its lifelong food is neither grass nor grain,
but nurture drawn from weeping balm and incense.
Its shroud, at last, is fume of nard and myrrh.
   The sinner, first, drops down as someone might
when grappled down, not knowing how, by demons
(or else some other epileptic turn),
   who then, on rising, gazes all around,

bewildered by the overwhelming ill
that came just now upon him, sighing, staring.

  So, too, this sinner, getting to his feet.
What power and might in God! How harsh it is!
How great the torrent of its vengeful blows!

  My leader then demanded who he was.
'I pelted down' – the sinner, in reply –
'to this wild gorge, right now, from Tuscany.

  Beast living suited me, not human life,
the mule that once I was. I'm Johnny Fucci,
animal. Pistoia is my proper hole.'

  I to my leader: 'Tell him, "Don't rush off!"
and make him say what guilt has thrust him down.
I've seen him. He's a man of blood and wrath.'

  The sinner, hearing this, made no pretence.
He fixed on me a concentrated eye,
and coloured up in brash embarrassment.

  'It pisses me right off,' he then declared,
'far more than being ripped away from life,
that you have got to see me in this misery.

  I can't say "no" to what you ask of me.
I'm stuck down here so deep 'cos it was me,
the thief who nicked the silver from the sanctuary.

  Then I just lied – to grass up someone else.
You won't, however, laugh at seeing this.
If ever you return from these dark dives,

  prick up your ears and hear my prophecy:
Pistoia first will slim and lose its Blacks.
Then Florence, too, renews its laws and ranks.

  Mars draws up fireballs from the Val di Magra,

wrapped all around in clouds and turbulence.
And these, in acrid, ever-driven storms,
    will battle high above the Picene acre.
A rapid bolt will rend the clouds apart,
and every single White be seared by wounds.
    I tell you this. I want it all to hurt.'

Canto XXXIII

TRAITORS TO NATION AND TRAITORS TO GUESTS

Jaws lifted now from that horrible dish,
the sinner – wiping clean each lip on hair that fringed
the mess he'd left the head in, at its rear –

began: 'You ask that I should tell anew
the pain that hopelessly, in thought alone,
before I voice it, presses at my heart.

Yet if I may, by speaking, sow the fruit
of hate to slur this traitor, caught between my teeth,
then words and tears, you'll see, will flow as one.

Who you might be, I do not know, nor how
you've come to be down here. But when you speak,
you seem (there's little doubt) a Florentine.

You need to see: I was Count Ugolino.
This is Ruggieri, the archbishop, there.
I'll tell you now why we two are so close.

That I, in consequence of his vile thoughts,
was captured – though I trusted in this man –
and after died, I do not need to say.

But this cannot have carried to your ears:
that is, how savagely I met my death.
You'll hear it now, and know if he has injured me.

One scant slit in the walls of Eaglehouse
(because of me, they call it now the Hunger Tower.
Be sure, though: others will be locked up there)

had shown me, in the shaft that pierces it,

many new moons by now, when this bad dream
tore wide the veil of what my future was.

This thing here then appeared to me as Master
of the Hounds, who tracked the wolf – his cubs as well –
out on the hill where Lucca hides from Pisa.

In front, as leaders of the pack, he placed
the clans Gualandi, Sismond and Lanfranchi,
their bitches hunting eager, lean and smart.

The chase was brief. Father and sons, it seemed,
were wearying; and soon – or so it seemed –
I saw those sharp fangs raking down their flanks.

I woke before the day ahead had come,
and heard my sons (my little ones were there)
cry in their sleep and call out for some food.

How hard you are if, thinking what my heart
foretold, you do not feel the pain of it.
Whatever will you weep for, if not that?

By now they all had woken up. The time
was due when, as routine, our food was brought.
Yet each was doubtful, thinking of their dream.

Listening, I heard the door below locked shut,
then nailed in place against that dreadful tower.
I looked in their dear faces, spoke no word.

I did not weep. Inward, I turned to stone.
They wept. And then my boy Anselmo spoke:
"What are you staring at? Father, what's wrong?"

And so I held my tears in check and gave
no answer all that day, nor all the night
that followed on, until another sun came up.

A little light had forced a ray into

43

our prison, so full of pain. I now could see
on all four faces my own expression.

Out of sheer grief, I gnawed on both my hands.
And they – who thought I did so from an urge
to eat – all, on the instant, rose and said:

"Father, for us the pain would be far less
if you would chose to eat us. You, having dressed us
in this wretched flesh, ought now to strip it off."

So I kept still, to not increase their miseries.
And that day and the day beyond, we all were mute.
Hard, cruel earth, why did you not gape wide?

As then we reached the fourth of all those days,
Gaddo pitched forward, stretching at my feet.
"Help me," he said. "Why don't you help me, Dad!"

And there he died. You see me here. So I saw them,
the three remaining, falling one by one
between the next days – five and six – then let

myself, now blind, feel over them, calling
on each, now all were dead, for two days more.
Then hunger proved a greater power than grief.'

His words were done. Now, eyes askew, he grabbed
once more that miserable skull – his teeth,
like any dog's teeth, strong against the bone.

Pisa, you scandal of the lovely land
where 'yes' is uttered in the form of *sì,*
your neighbours may be slow to punish you,

but let those reefs, Capraia and Gorgogna,
drift, as a barrage, to the Arno's mouth,
so that your people – every one – are drowned.

So what if – as the rumour goes – the great Count

Ugolino did cheat fortresses from you.
You had no right to crucify his children.

    Pisa, you are a newborn Thebes! Those boys
were young. That made them innocent. I've named
just two. I now name Uguiccione and Brigata.

    We now moved on, and came to where the ice
so roughly swaddled yet another brood.
And these – not hunched – bend back for all to view.

    They weep. Yet weeping does not let them weep.
Their anguish meets a blockage at the eye.
Turned in, this only makes their heartache more.

    Their tears first cluster into frozen buds,
and then – as though a crystal visor – fill
the socket of the eye beneath each brow.

    My own face now – a callus in the chill –
had ceased to be a throne to any kind
of sentiment. And yet, in spite of all,

    it seemed I felt a wind still stirring here.
'Who moves these currents, sir?' I now inquired.
'At depths like these, aren't vapours wholly spent?'

    He in reply: 'Come on, come on! You soon
will stand where your own probing eye shall see
what brings this drizzling exhalation on.'

    A case of icy-eye-scab now yelled out:
'You must be souls of such malignancy
you merit placement in the lowest hole.

    Prise off this rigid veil, to clear my eyes.
Let me awhile express the grief that swells
in my heart's womb before my tears next freeze.'

    I answered: 'Are you asking help from me?

Tell me who you are. Then I'll free your gaze,
or travel – promise! – to the deepest ice.'

'I,' he replied, 'am Brother Alberigo,
I of the Evil Orchard, Fruiterer.
Here I receive exquisite dates for figs.'

'Oh,' I now said, 'so you're already dead?'
'Well, how my body fares above,' he said,
'still in the world, my knowledge is not sure.

There is, in Ptolomea, this advantage,
that souls will frequently come falling down
before Fate Atropos has granted them discharge.

I very willingly will tell you more,
but only scrape this tear glaze from my face.
The instant any soul commits, like me,

some act of treachery, a demon takes
possession of that body-form and rules
its deeds until its time is done. Swirling,

the soul runs downwards to this sink. And so
the body of that shade behind – a-twitter
all this winter through – still seems up there, perhaps.

You're bound to know, arriving only now,
that this is Signor Branca ("Hookhand") d'Oria.
Years have gone by since he was ice-packed here.'

'I think,' I said, 'that this must be a con.
For how can Branca d'Oria be dead?
He eats and drinks and sleeps and puts his clothes on.'

'Recall that ditch,' he said, 'named Rotklorsville,
where, higher up, they brew adhesive pitch?
Well, long before Mike Zanche got to that,

Hookhand was history. He, as proxy, left

a devil in his skin (his kinsman's here as well,
the one who planned with him the double-cross).

    But please, now reach your hand to me down here.
Open my eyes for me.' I did not open them.
To be a swine in this case was pure courtesy.

    You Genovese, deviant, deranged
and stuffed with every sort of vicious canker!
Why have you not been wiped yet from the earth?

    Among the worst of all the Romagnuoli
I found there one of yours, whose works were such
his soul already bathes in Cocytus.

    His body, seemingly, lives on above.

Canto XXXIV

TRAITORS TO BENEFACTORS

'*Vexilla regis prodeunt inferni*,
marching towards us. Fix your eyes ahead,'
my teacher said, 'and see if you can see it.'
    As though a windmill when a thick fog breathes –
or else when dark night grips our hemisphere –
seen from a distance, turning in the wind,
    so there a great contraption had appeared.
And I now shrank, against the wind, behind
my guide. There were no glades to shelter in.
    I was by now (I write this verse in fear)
where all the shades in ice were covered up,
transparent as are straws preserved in glass.
    Some lay there flat, and some were vertical,
one with head raised, another soles aloft,
another like a bow, bent face to feet.
    And then when we had got still further on,
where now my master chose to show to me
that creature who had once appeared so fair,
    he drew away from me and made me stop,
saying: 'Now see! Great Dis! Now see the place
where you will need to put on all your strength.'
    How weak I now became, how faded, dry –
reader, don't ask, I shall not write it down –
for anything I said would fall far short.
    I neither died nor wholly stayed alive.

Just think yourselves, if your minds are in flower,
what I became, bereft of life and death.

The emperor of all these realms of gloom
stuck from the ice at mid-point on his breast.
And I am more a giant (to compare)
    than any giant measured to his arm.
So now you'll see how huge the whole must be,
when viewed in fit proportion to that limb.

If, once, he was as lovely as now vile,
when first he raised his brow against his maker,
then truly grief must all proceed from him.

How great a wonder it now seemed to me
to see three faces on a single head!
The forward face was brilliant vermilion.

The other two attached themselves to that
along each shoulder on the central point,
and joined together at the crest of hair.

The rightward face was whitish, dirty yellow.
The left in colour had the tint of those
beyond the source from which the Nile first swells.

Behind each face there issued two great vanes,
all six proportioned to a fowl like this.
I never saw such size in ocean sails.

Not feathered as a bird's wings are, bat-like
and leathery, each fanned away the air,
so three unchanging winds moved out from him,
    Cocytus being frozen hard by these.
He wept from all six eyes. And down each chin
both tears and bloody slobber slowly ran.

In every mouth he mangled with his teeth

(as flax combs do) a single sinning soul,
but brought this agony to three at once.

Such biting, though, affects the soul in front
as nothing to the scratching he received.
His spine at times showed starkly, bare of skin.

'That one up there, condemned to greater pain,
is Judas Iscariot,' my teacher said,
'his head inside, his feet out, wriggling hard.

The other two, their heads hung down below,
are Brutus, dangling from the jet black snout
(look how he writhes there, uttering not a word!),

the other Cassius with his burly look.
But night ascends once more. And now it's time
for us to quit this hole. We've seen it all.'

As he desired, I clung around his neck.
With purpose, he selected time and place
and, when the wings had opened to the full,

he took a handhold on the furry sides,
and then, from tuft to tuft, he travelled down
between the shaggy pelt and frozen crust.

But then, arriving where the thigh bone turns
(the hips extended to their widest there),
my leader, with the utmost stress and strain,

swivelled his head to where his shanks had been
and clutched the pelt like someone on a climb,
so now I thought: 'We're heading back to Hell.'

'Take care,' my teacher said. 'By steps like these,'
breathless and panting, seemingly all-in,
'we need to take our leave of so much ill.'

Then through a fissure in that rock he passed

and set me down to perch there on its rim.
After, he stretched his careful stride towards me.

Raising my eyes, I thought that I should see
Lucifer where I, just now, had left him,
but saw instead his legs held upwards there.

If I was struggling then to understand,
let other dimwits think how they'd have failed
to see what point it was that I now passed.

'Up on your feet!' my teacher ordered me.
'The way is long, the road is cruelly hard.
The sun is at the morning bell already.'

This was no stroll, where now we had arrived,
through any palace but a natural cave.
The ground beneath was rough, the light was weak.

'Before my roots are torn from this abyss,
sir,' I said, upright, 'to untangle me
from error, say a little more of this.

Where is the ice? And why is that one there
fixed upside down? How is it that the sun
progressed so rapidly from evening on to day?'

And he in answer: 'You suppose you're still
on that side of the centre where I gripped
that wormrot's coat that pierces all the world.

While I was still descending, you were there.
But once I turned, you crossed, with me, the point
to which from every part all weight drags down.

So you stand here beneath the hemisphere
that now is covered wholly with dry land,
under the highest point at which there died
    the one man sinless in his birth and life.

Your feet are set upon a little sphere
that forms the other aspect of Giudecca.

It's morning here. It's evening over there.
The thing that made a ladder of his hair
is still as fixed as he has always been.

Falling from Heaven, when he reached this side,
the lands that then spread out to southern parts
in fear of him took on a veil of sea.

These reached our hemisphere. Whatever now
is visible to us – in flight perhaps from him –
took refuge here and left an empty space.'

There is a place (as distant from Beelzebub
as his own tomb extends in breadth)
known not by sight but rather by the sound

of waters falling in a rivulet
eroding, by the winding course it takes (which is
not very steep), an opening in that rock.

So now we entered on that hidden path,
my lord and I, to move once more towards
a shining world. We did not care to rest.

We climbed, he going first and I behind,
until through some small aperture I saw
the lovely things the skies above us bear.

Now we came out, and once more saw the stars.